Jamal Gerald

IDOL

OBERON BOOKS
LONDON
WWW.OBERONBOOKS.COM

First published in 2020 by Oberon Books Ltd
521 Caledonian Road, London N7 9RH
Tel: +44 (0) 20 7607 3637 / Fax: +44 (0) 20 7607 3629
e-mail: info@oberonbooks.com
www.oberonbooks.com

PB ISBN: 9781786828590
E ISBN: 9781786828583

Cover image: The Other Richard
Cover design: Rabbit Hole

Printed and bound in the UK

Visit www.oberonbooks.com to read more about all our books and to buy them. You will also find features, author interviews and news of any author events, and you can sign up for e-newsletters and be the first to hear about our new releases.

Printed on FSC accredited paper

10 9 8 7 6 5 4 3 2 1

Contents

Foreword

It is only right that I juxtapose my reflections on Jamal Gerald's remarkable *Idol* with the gospel of an idol of my own.

Black skin,

When the second wave feminists declared that the personal was political, they took a triangle, and claimed it consisted of two sides only.

black braids,

But they missed a trick. Always, the personal and political are joined by the spiritual: and all three are channelled through the body.

Black waves,

At their most compelling, transformative and powerful, spiritual practices demand that we grow as people, that we bring the best of all we have into the world, and offer it to the ecosystems and communities of which we are a part. We simultaneously root ourselves in the body and the earth and transcend such concerns.

black days,

When correctly applied, the spiritual demands justice of the political, and gives the personal a resonance beyond death. The political grounds the spiritual in reality and holds the personal accountable. The personal turns the spiritual into tangible ritual, and troubles the political with our fragility and our failures.

Black baes,

You need all three, and they must be *embodied.*

black days

The last performance of Jamal's that I experienced was *FADoubleGOT.*

What I am most struck by as I sit in *Idol* is that such growth has taken place since then.

Spiritual growth, political growth, artistic growth. Growth in how he positions himself, and how he speaks about his relationship with his mother. Desires obscured in the earlier show are now agonisingly frank in this one. Hesitant movement has blossomed into full on routines, with the expertise that comes from growing up with rhythm, recreating dance moves you learn in the club and mimicking music videos in the living room while your mum's at work. Hip hop is delivered with a dexterity that is unmistakeable to those of us that learnt how to rap from CDs, tapes and illegally downloaded mp3s. A stark DIY aesthetic is fully realised now, transformed into an all-encompassing space of ritual, teetering on the edge of being an installation.

These are black-owned things

Idol oscillates between the sacred and the profane.

We are cleansing ourselves in holy water and day dreaming orgies in the church

We are bickering in the school playground and stanning on the internet

We are making offerings to our gods and scrubbing homes in ammonia

We are disrupting award ceremonies and singing along to pop music about heartbreak.

This contrast is perhaps at its most beautiful when we end the show in the domestic space. The ritual of a parent doing a child's hair, and the dreams of an elder brother for his younger sibling are one of the foundational images of the beauty of blackness, of the safe spaces we create for ourselves away from the white gaze.

This same contrast is at its most delicious: truffle rich, velvet decadent and lemon fresh when he swan dives into blasphemy. Jamal's twitter bio announces that he likes to cause trouble, and in *Idol* he delivers on that promise to thrilling effect.

Black faith

What were the routes of religion? What was it feeding?

Jamal refuses to leave his spiritual health in the hands of White Jesus.

When Jamal positions internalised anti-blackness as a curse placed on him by those that want to harm his family, he elevates the slick, dubious realm of the psychic. Its associations with public access TV, early 90s Whoopi Goldberg and neon lights shifts into the realm of the political. Ancestral political legacy becomes personal spite becomes hex.

still can't be washed away

What are the roots of stan culture? What do we need that it gives to us?

Jamal does not easily leave his political agency with black capitalists either, as he traces the real baulk of their wealth back to white men.

This lingers in his personal too, as he traces the old lovers who turn away from his caught feelings back to white men, and white wealth also. In her autobiography 'We're Going to Need More Wine' Gabrielle Union reminds her readers that you cannot self-esteem your way out of how the world treats you. It is an aching truth, and one that reappears frequently in Jamal's work.

Not even in that Florida water

Idol lives in the messy realities of real life. It is constrained by practicalities, and the limits of freedom in a world riddled with violence and unhealed wounds. Beyoncé can't set him free any more than street evangelists can: but the first offers him pleasure, and that is a power in and of itself.

Not even in that Florida water

But it is not only Jamal who has grown in the interim between *FADoubleGOT* and *Idol*. He has gone one better and demanded that spirituality – or at least our diasporic understanding of it – also grows, and that what we consider sacred broadens out. It is a lover that brings Jamal to the rituals that weave *Idol* together. Jamal has been searching for someone who will see themselves in him, in who he will see himself. That the two of them might see the spiritual in each other and love, ecstatically.

In that Florida water

for colored girls who have considered suicide / when the rainbow is enuf, Ntozake Shange's 1976 masterpiece, ends in ecstasy:
   'i found god in myself / & i loved her / I loved her fiercely'
Jamal leaves us on a similar note.

He may have had to journey to the Caribbean to find the love that he deserves, but in *Idol* he brings this home and shares it with us, his audience, his fellow melenated ones.

I cannot thank him enough.

Selina Thompson
January 2020

Author's Note

I remember how I felt when I rarely saw myself when studying at Leeds Beckett University.

The majority of the curriculum was white. I and one of my best friends Alicia were the only Black people in the class. It was a feeling I hated, as you can imagine. It's something that I didn't want any other aspiring Black artists to feel. I promised myself that I would make as much work as possible, so Black students could see my work but mostly see themselves represented. And since then, a Black student said she saw *Idol*, wrote an essay on it and got a first. Yay!

I was interested in exploring these questions: What happens when you see Black representation? What happens when you don't see it? Well, for starters, if I don't see any melanated people I lose interest quite quickly. Going to a Catholic Church was already boring, but maybe it might have been slightly more engaging if the icons had had my skin tone.

I'm obsessed with pop culture. Yes, I know, I'm stating the obvious. The research period for this show was my most exciting by far. I always found pop culture to be a great way to talk about complex topics such as race. Even better – an accessible way, because there is an aspect of pop culture that most people engage with. If you bring up a film that's troublesome due to its stereotypical portrayals of Black people, to me, that's already a more compelling way to discuss racism.

There are so many Black people in this world that have issues with their complexion and Black features, and that's something that makes me teary. I made this work for Black audiences, with the intention to encourage Black people to continue taking up space and loving their Blackness.

After a performance, an audience member said: 'I'm really happy with being Black now.' It's quite bittersweet. Because I'm sad he didn't love his Blackness before, but I'm humbled my show helped him find happiness for being Black. His comment is something that will always stay with me, and I believe it shows the importance of Black representation.

Jamal Gerald
January 2020

Acknowledgements

Special thanks to my Family: My Mummy, Winifred Gerald, my sister, Celeste, and my brother, Déshaun, for always showing me love and being an inspiration in my work.

Thanks to my creative and production team, I don't know what I would've done without all of you. Maddy (my ride or die), Rachael, Pariss, Azizi, Ben, Charlotte, Helen, Stella, Hannah and Akeim. You're all gems and will forever have a place in my heart. Thanks for coming on this journey with me.

Thanks to Amy Letman (Transform) and Richard Warburton (Theatre in the Mill) for commissioning the show. You're both the best! Thanks for believing in me and for continuing to support my work. Shout out to Leeds Inspired, hÅb, STUN and Contact for investing in the show too! Thanks to the ones that gave me feedback on my ideas: Arielle John, Zodwa Nyoni, Rheima Robinson, Nwando Ebizie and Max Omamogho.

Thanks to Louise Jones for the voice lessons. I really needed them because I was struggling, haha. Thanks to Toni-Dee Paul for hosting the Post Show Salons. Thanks to Lauren Lister for making the work more accessible with her BSL interpretations. Thanks to Awo Efuwape Andall for the prayers and epigrams for the Orisas.

Thanks to The Other Richard, JMA Photography, Fresh Label and Ndrika Anyika for making me look so good. Thanks to Sophie Bradey for being so supportive throughout the process. Thanks to Selina Thompson and MindMove Counselling for helping me to look after my mental health. Thanks to Oberon for publishing the text.

Thanks to Alice Yard, EAST YARD, Arts Council England and the British Council for the research trip to Trinidad and Tobago! To every Black person that has engaged with this work, thank you! And to the Orisas, thank you for coming into my life and for guiding me throughout this creative process.

Idol premiered at Transform 19 at Prime Studios, Leeds, on 27 April 2019.

Written and performed by Jamal Gerald

CREATIVE TEAM
Musician/Performer **Pariss Elektra**
Musician/Performer **Azizi Cole**
Dramaturge **Maddy Costa**
Outside Eye **Rachael Young**
Movement Director **Akeim Toussaint Buck**
Stage and Lighting **Ben Pacey**
Costume **Hannah Wilson**
Ritual Consultant **Christella Litras**
Stage Manager **Charlotte Woods**
Production Manager **Helen Mugridge**
Producer **Transform**

A Jamal Gerald, Transform and Theatre in the Mill Co-Production. Seed commissioned by hÅb, STUN and Contact for Works Ahead. Supported by Leeds Inspired, part of Leeds City Council, and using public funding from the National Lottery through Arts Council England.
www.jamalgerald.com

DATES

2019

27th–28th April, Transform 19, Leeds

25th May, Theatre in the Mill, Bradford

2020

11th–15th February, NOW 20, The Yard, London

28th February, Derby Theatre

13th–14th March, MAC, Birmingham

19th–21st March, Royal Exchange Theatre, Manchester

8th–9th April, Sheffield Theatres

7th May, Cambridge Junction

11th May, caravan showcase, Brighton Festival

22nd–23rd May, Leeds Playhouse

Jamal Gerald

Jamal Gerald is an artist based in Leeds. His work is conversational, socially conscious, a celebration of individuality and focuses on identity and lived experiences. Jamal mostly makes the type of work that he wants to see, with the aim of taking up space as a Black queer person.

He has made work for poetry slams, films, parties, cafes and theatres. He was also a co-deviser and performer for Scottee's critically acclaimed *Putting Words in Your Mouth*, which premiered at the Roundhouse in November 2016. In 2018, he was awarded Arts Council England's Artists' International Development Fund to do research in Trinidad and Tobago. Jamal's work has also been shown at Kampnagel (Hamburg), SPILL Festival of Performance, Leeds Playhouse, Battersea Arts Centre and the Barbican.

Pariss Elektra

Pariss Elektra is a singer-songwriter and multi-instrumentalist from London. She studied Jazz and Popular Music at Leeds College of Music. Now based in Leeds, Pariss is constantly performing around West Yorkshire solo, in duos and full bands. Pariss is a force of nature when singing and especially whilst playing percussion instruments. Recently she had a residency at a stylish, not-so-secret club called *The Domino*, singing lead vocals, playing guitar and percussion in *The Sugar Rays Experience* on a Saturday night every fortnight. She is also one of the lead singers in a group called *New Position*, a product of the members' joint love for J-Dilla and Prince. Pariss Elektra is an excellent master of ceremonies, always delivering a high-frequency performance guaranteed to give you a shot of pure joy.

Azizi Cole

Raised in Handsworth, Birmingham, music has always been a key influencer in Azizi's life. Coming from a dance background he was always fixated with the connection between the two art forms and how different listening experiences can induce the way we move, from live to pre-recorded music. Since then he has continued his development as a composer and accompanist for dance, live composing in technique classes for multiple institutions such as Phoenix Dance Theatre, Northern School of Contemporary Dance and Rambert since 2015. He has also been commissioned to compose for various performances as well as teaching musicality workshops as an independent freelancer.

Maddy Costa

Maddy Costa is a writer and dramaturg interested in opening space for conversation through and around performance. Artists she has worked with as dramaturg include Selina Thompson, Paula Varjack, Rhiannon Armstrong, and Harry Josephine Giles. She contributes reviews to online magazine *Exeunt* and works closely with theatre-makers including Sheila Ghelani, Unfolding Theatre and Fuel to create unusual documentation of their work. With Mary Paterson and Diana Damian Martin she is co-founder and co-host of *Something Other* and the *Department of Feminist Conversations*, inter-related platforms for experimental writing, dialogue and critical thinking. She is co-writing a partial map of contemporary performance with Andy Field, to be published by Oberon in 2020. She co-hosts a pop-up theatre club – like a book group, but for performance – across London.

Rachael Young

Rachael Young's interdisciplinary performance practice exists on the boundaries between live art, dance, contemporary theatre and socially engaged projects; creating spaces for intersectional realities to be explored and celebrated and for alternative narratives and forms to evolve and be heard. Rachael's recent shows, *OUT*, won 2017 South East Dance A Space to Dance Brighton Fringe Award and was nominated for the Total Theatre & The Place Award for Dance 2017, and *NIGHTCLUBBING* was nominated for a 2019 Total Theatre Award for Innovation, Experimentation & Playing with Form. Rachael is the recipient of the inaugural Eclipse Award and was named an Artist to Watch 2019 by the British Council. Rachael's work is shown in the UK and internationally including at: Skopje Pride (Skopje), Live Collision Festival (Dublin), RIGHTABOUTNOW (Amsterdam), Theatre de L'Usine (Geneva), TRANSFORM! #3 (Marseille), ImPulsTanz (Vienna International Dance Festival), The Place, Tate Modern, and Battersea Arts Centre.

Akeim Toussaint Buck

Akeim is a multifaceted performing artist and maker, born in Jamaica and raised in England.

He seeks to create moving, thought-provoking, accessible and free-spirited projects with a myriad of art forms. Since graduating from the Northern School of Contemporary Dance with a first-class honours Bachelor degree in Performing Arts, Akeim has been involved in cross disciplinary projects working with a wide range of artists from around the world. His focus as a maker, collaborator and performer is to combine expressive skills such as dance, poetry, beat-box, singing and acting to create performances, telling stories that galvanise diverse audiences.

Ben Pacey

Ben's recent lighting design includes Verity Standen's *Undersong*; Sleepdogs' *Dark Land Light House*; *Ice Road* for Raucous; *Thrive* for Zest Theatre; *Getting Dressed* for Second Hand Dance; Uninvited Guests' *This Last Tempest*; Kiln Ensemble's *The Furies*; and Melanie Wilson's *Autobiographer*. He also designs for performance; recent credits include *Idol* for Jamal Gerald, *Vessel* for Sue Maclaine, *Not I* for Touretteshero; *This Restless State* for Fuel; *Delightful* for Birmingham Rep/Kiln Ensemble; Greg Wohead's *Comeback Special*; Javaad Alipoor's *The Believers Are But Brothers*. As an artist/maker, Ben makes installations, animations, and writes performance texts. He co-directs Dens & Signals (*Animals!*, *Feast of the Dead*, *The Wake*, *A Thousand Shards of Glass*). He's an associate artist of Coney.

Hannah Wilson

Hannah Wilson is a stylist and creative based in the North of England. She studied at Leeds College of Art before continuing her undergraduate studies at Goldsmiths, University of London, gaining a degree in Design. Hannah has previously worked on independent theatre projects with the Leeds based festival, Transform. Previous credits include: *The Darkest Corners* (RashDash), *bYOB* (70/30 Split) and *Idol* (Jamal Gerald). She also works across TV, Film and commercial advertising as an Art Director and Designer.

Christella Litras

Christella Litras is a singer-songwriter, producer, vocal arranger, composer and keyboardist. During her final year of study at Leeds University, she worked with Geraldine Connor on her project *Carnival Messiah* and went on to represent Carnival Messiah in Trinidad at the World Carnival Conference. After university, she pursued her passion for live music, performing as part of Rihanna's backing band and performing as a support act for Jamiroquai and Beverley Knight during their Japan and UK tours respectively. Between 2000-2004, she revisited Trinidad, working on four studio projects with established World Music and recording artist Ella Andall and joined her trans-Caribbean tour performing for Nelson Mandela. In 2007, she initiated her own Vocal Performance group Caution Collective, with the aim of developing talented young singers and providing them with performance opportunities. The group continues to thrive, performing to sell-out audiences in Leeds.

Charlotte Woods

Charlotte Woods trained at the Royal Welsh College of Music and Drama, now based in Leeds where she works freelance as a Venue Technician, Production Manager, Lighting Designer, and Technical Stage Manager. Charlotte works with artists across many disciplines and prefers working with independent artists or smaller creative teams to closely engage and collaborate with performers to realise their creative and technical needs. Having worked with Jamal previously on a tour of *Dogmatic*, Charlotte was thrilled to be a part of the creative team that delivered *Idol*. Recent projects: *Joygernaut* (Andy Craven-Griffiths), *WOKE* (Testament), *Bed* (Performance Ensemble), *Bird's Nest Billy* (Fidget Theatre), *Where We Began* (SBC Theatre), *LOVE SONG* (Kenber & Son), *TANJA* (SBC Theatre), *Motherload* (Grace Surman). Charlotte has also worked as a freelance Venue Technician for art spaces across Yorkshire including: Yorkshire Dance, Trouble At Mill, The Constitutional, Theatre in the Mill and Centre for Live Art Yorkshire.

Helen Mugridge

Helen is an experienced stage and production manager. Her previous credits include: *RED*, Likely Story (Wales Millennium Centre), *Gaping Hole*, Rachel Mars and Greg Wohead

(Ovalhouse, London), *Little Wimmin*, Figs in Wigs (Pleasance, London), *Class*, Scottee (Edinburgh and UK tour), *Les Voyages*, Company XY (Greenwich and Docklands International Festival), *Call it a Day*, Greg Wohead (Tour), *Atomic 50*, interactive installation for Waltham Forest Borough of Culture, *Idol*, Jamal Gerald (Transform 19, Leeds and Theatre in the Mill, Bradford), *Night Tree*, Secondhanddance (South East Tour), *I'm A Phoenix, Bitch*, Bryony Kimmings (Grand Hall, BAC and International dates), *Fat Blokes*, Scottee (UK tour), *Mirabel*, Chris Goode & Co (Ovalhouse), *Oranges and Elephants*, Lil Warren and Susie McKenna (Hoxton Hall), *The Shape of the Pain*, Rachel Bagshaw and Chris Thorpe with Chinaplate, (Edinburgh, Germany, BAC), *Golem*, 1927 (West End, UK and International tour).

Transform

Transform is a producing company and biennial international performance festival based in Leeds. Each festival assembles some of the boldest artists from across the North of England and the globe, travelling through iconic venues across the city. Recent commissioning and production credits include *Idol* by Jamal Gerald, *The Believers Are But Brothers* by Javaad Alipoor, *The Darkest Corners* by RashDash and *WANTED* by Chris Goode & Company. Transform is the leader of the Creative Europe network 'Festivals of the Future' supporting founder and female-led festivals across Europe, and works consistently to bring some of the most high quality and daring international performance to Leeds and the wider UK.

www.transformfestival.org

Theatre in the Mill

Theatre in the Mill is a Bradford-based performance venue and artist development space situated on the University of Bradford campus. Collaborating with artists on work reflecting their three core goals of Representation, Inclusion and Innovation, they are committed to presenting, developing and supporting socially responsible and innovative performance across a range of art forms. They strive to create spaces that promote dialogue, and art that represents the narrative of the people, the city and the region. They believe in the need for audiences to see themselves represented and portrayed in contemporary culture and that they have a responsibility to be a mirror that reflects the lives of those around them.

www.theatreinthemill.com

For my fellow melanated ones

Iba Prayer

Olodumare Mojuba
Olorun Mojuba
Orun Mojuba
Irunmole Mojuba
Igba Irunmole Ojukutun Mojuba
Igba Irunmole Ojukosin Mojuba
Aiye Mojuba
Omi Mojuba
Ina Mojuba
Afefe Mojuba
Egun Mojuba
Awon Iyaami Mojuba
Ori Mojuba
Oluwo Mojuba
Ejubona Mojuba
Gbogbo Orisa Mojuba.
Ase Ase Ase Olodumare.

In the Palais, there is a large drop cloth that shapes the space with multi-coloured streamers.

A red arch with red altar shelves, there are burning candles on the first shelf and a framed picture of Black Jesus above it.

An altar table is in the centre of the Palais. It has a white cloth on top of it, with multi-coloured streamers around it, a statue of a white Jesus, shea butter, incense and burning candles.

There are framed pictures of celebrities. From left to right:

Freddie Mercury, Prince, Frank Ocean, Lil' Kim, Beyoncé and Kendrick Lamar.

Four Orisa altars: A black and red one for Esu, a yellow one for Osun, a red and white one for Sango, and a purple one for Oya.

Each altar has a picture of an Orisa, candles, flowers, incense and a white plate with an offering. A black candle and incense are burning for Esu.

ESU

Spirit of the Cross Roads.
He who has perforated ears so he can hear all prayers and petitions.
The Divine Messenger of Transformation.
One who guards our free will.

Ajibike ma se mi o. Esu ma se mi o.
Mo Rubio Esu Opin o. Ase.

The ritual opens. JAMAL is praying to Esu. The audience has rose water poured into their hands before entering the Palais. PARISS and AZIZI are chanting 'Elegba 'go (ko) Lona' (Make Way for Esu, Orisa of the Cross Road) by Ella Andall.

They're asking Esu to open the doors to the spiritual world.

Once the audience is seated, JAMAL picks up a glass bottle, he then takes a sip and sprays the space with rum. He crosses the space, visiting each altar. Once JAMAL is finished he goes back into a praying position. AZIZI and PARISS both finish performing the chant, they get up and meet JAMAL to do an Orisa greet. PARISS and AZIZI then greet each other and sit.

JAMAL sits down and begins to tell a story.

My mother has always told me that if I come home late, I need to walk in anti-clockwise. This was to prevent anyone coming inside the house with me. If you don't want anyone to follow you once you leave this space, I suggest you do the same.

My mother is the superstitious type. This is mostly because she grew up in a village called Trials in Montserrat, in the East Caribbean. And Trials is now a bit of a ghost town. It has ashes which spin, levitate and reminisce about the people that once lived on the island. Half of the island is now restricted due to the volcanic eruptions. On the other half, people still have the chance to skip round the black sand beaches, and embrace the charming winks from the Sun.

Even though my mother left Montserrat at the age of sixteen, her upbringing hasn't left her, especially the superstitions, which have been passed down to me. If she was ever worried about any spirits, she would scrub down parts of the house with ammonia, whilst cussing the evil spirits out in patois. My mother makes up her own sayings, so when she cusses, she'll say things like 'Yah pussyclart rarse hole.' She told me she does this to help bring harmony into the house, to block out evil spirits, and to prevent any type of possession from happening.

She takes Caribbean superstitions really seriously. When you sneeze a lot someone is talking about you. This is also the case if your ear is burning. If it's the right ear, they're speaking highly of you. And if it's the left, they're not. They're probably plotting something against you.

If there's a spider sitting on the top of your wall, that means you'll be getting some money soon. This is also the same if your palms are itchy. Never put shoes on the bed, you'll get bad luck.

If your left eye is jumping, that means something bad is going to happen. If your right eye is jumping, that means you'll see someone that you haven't seen in a long time. Also a cold shiver means someone is walking over your grave, and there's plenty more.

Even though I do laugh at my mother and other family members, I have found myself taking some of the superstitions quite seriously, like whenever my left eye jumps, I'm always on edge. Creating melodramatic scenarios in my head, but then they never happen.

My mother went from Leeds to Wolverhampton to see a psychic once, who told her that my family is cursed and that some evil people were going to try and kill her. Because of this, my mother made me go into the bath, which was filled with purple liquid. And then I had to hold rosary beads and repeat a psalm three times in order to protect myself. After this, I had to light some incense in my room, say a psalm in the morning and at night.

PARISS and AZIZI play improvised music.

JAMAL chants the Psalm dutifully but ironically.

Psalm 140

Save me, Lord, from evildoers;
keep me safe from violent people.
They are always plotting evil,
always stirring up quarrels.
Their tongues are like deadly snakes;
their words are like a cobra's poison.
Protect me, Lord, from the power of the wicked;
keep me safe from violent people
who plot my downfall.
The proud have set a trap for me;
they have laid their snares,
and along the path they have set traps to catch me.

PARISS and AZIZI stop playing.

And all of this happened in my final year of university.
My mother made me do this as an adult, at twenty-one
years old. Even at my age of twenty-five, she still asks for my
assistance in scrubbing down the house with ammonia.

*

When I was young, I would have to go to Church most
Sundays, and I always felt uncomfortable. There have been
times where I've been stopped by religious people who
would try and save me. Anyone from people on the street,
cleaners and taxi drivers. They could probably sense that I
like men and thought that I needed Jesus or Allah.

One time, a Black woman stopped me in the street and asked if I believed in Jesus? I said yes, I'm Catholic. She said 'Well, I'm sorry, honey, but being Catholic is not going to get you a place in heaven.' She went on to question what has Mary ever done for me and then explained that it should only be Jesus who is praised. So that's one thing that put me off of going to Church, people trying to save me. And there was also a feeling in my spirit telling me that something isn't right about this holy place. It was like I was getting a warning from my ancestors.

Whenever I was in Church, I would stare at some good looking men to pass the time. I'd imagine pouring holy water onto them, having an orgy, fucking each other like porn stars whilst baby Jesus and Mary watch over us.

'It Bend Like Banana' by Vybz Kartel plays.

JAMAL starts touching his body, whining up his waist and grinding on the floor – continuing even when the music stops.

Yeah, I was one of those Catholic boys. A Black male queer version of Madonna, or maybe I was a child of Judas? But no one in Church would ever know. I went through confirmation, so I could make my first communion to receive the body and blood of Christ. My confirmation name is Joseph, and I did all of this because my mother wanted me to.

I never lit a candle in Church. I would light a candle
for my favourite celebrities, before ever lighting one for
any saints.

JAMAL puts on a Prince-inspired outfit.

PARISS and AZIZI start performing 'Let's Go Crazy' by Prince.

JAMAL dances with a microphone in his hand.

Pop culture was my true religion and Black and queer
celebrities were my saints, or better yet, my deities.

Album cover of Prince's 'LoveSexy' appears on projection.

Like His Royal Badness, Prince, a Black man doing
things that I never thought would be okay for a
Black man to do. Challenging the stereotype of Black
masculinity, from taking risks like wearing high heel boots,
exploring sexuality through his lyrics and eccentric live
performances, his flamboyant clothing, like his iconic
yellow jumpsuit outfit where his ass was out, and the way
he threw plenty of shade. He was such a rebel. And if I
were in a dramatic situation, I would ask myself, 'What
would Prince do?' before I would ever question 'What
would Jesus do?' He's one of the reasons why I now feel
it's okay to be my extra self. I thank him for being so bold,
brave, beautiful and Black.

They stop playing.

Prince once said:

'I can't be played. A person trying to play me plays themselves.'

When I was a kid, I dreamt of becoming a celebrity, so I could say cool things like that.

I wanted to walk the red carpet, camera flashes in time with each pose I strike. As I got older, I wanted to be in a power couple relationship with Frank Ocean. Who am I kidding? I would still love for that to happen. He's everything and more!

Pop culture was my way of escaping from all the fucked up things in my reality. If you didn't know, having idols is a sin. Oops. Whenever I went to Church, I was reminded that I was a sinner.

I liked sinning. It was fun, I always felt like I was just being myself whenever I sinned. It felt so good to be bad. And celebrities looked like a bunch of sinners to me.

There was a time where it was a duty to always watch award shows. It was important for me to know what was going on in celebrity culture. Even if I couldn't watch the whole show, I would make sure to see the highlights and I still do it now.

I remember watching the VMAs in 2009. My Queen Bey came and slayed the stage, as per usual. And I was so happy to see Britney Spears winning Best Pop Video. P!nk singing and flying in the air. Madonna's speech about Michael Jackson, followed by a tribute from his sister, Janet. Lady Gaga's blood filled performance, and then when Lil Mama came on stage to surprise both Jay Z and Alicia Keys. And the one thing I will never forget is this:

> *A video of Kanye West interrupting Taylor Swift at the VMAs in 2009 plays.*
>
> *JAMAL takes off his Prince outfit and puts on a T-shirt with a Black Madonna and baby Jesus. The video ends.*

I couldn't believe Kanye would do such a thing. Well, not really. He did say that George Bush doesn't care about Black people on live television. I felt so sorry for Taylor, because I would hate it if someone ever did that to me. Kanye reminds me of those friends that you love so much, but they're problematic as fuck. I can't talk, because I know I can be such a dick. Only within reason, of course.

> *JAMAL puts shea butter on his fingers and then rubs it on his forehead spreading it to the top of his head.*
>
> *He does this to honour his Ori.*
>
> *He lights incense and holds it whilst walking around the stage.*

I had a friend in high school called Akua. She would make fun of me and I would make fun of her. You know, good old banter. She would make fun of how big my nostrils were and how big my forehead is. And now everyone is looking at my forehead, lovely.

She would always tell me to shut up and close them caves. In return, I would call her dark chocolate, and I'm sure I called her a gorilla at one point too. There was a period, where she would ask people in our year group who they thought the darkest girl was. And when people said it was her, she always denied it and said that it was someone else.

And as the years went on, becoming more aware of white supremacy, the way it crawls and breathes into every little aspect of western society, I realised the jokes we exchanged were rooted in internalised anti-Blackness. Maybe this was the curse that the psychic was telling my mother about.

I started to notice anti-Blackness more, from arguing with a guy called Dwayne, about who is lighter between me and him. He was so happy when we realised it was him, I cut me eye.

I didn't realise my annoyance at first, but I look back now and I question where did it come from. Because I've never thought to myself *I wish I was lighter.*

And my friend Omari, who saw the back of my head, and said that I looked like a runaway slave, like a runaway slave, like a runaway slave just because my hair wasn't combed that day. It crawls and breathes.

OSUN

*Spirit of Mystery, Mother of Abundance, Mother of the Mirror/
Reflection (self),
Spirit of the River, Guardian of the Character of Women,
Spirit of Seduction, Mother of Dance, Loves Brass and Honey.*

JAMAL places the incense on the yellow altar.

He tastes some honey and then pours it onto five oranges.

He lights a yellow candle, rings a bell five times, closes his eyes briefly and opens them.

He then makes a beat with his hands and feet. AZIZI and PARISS join in with singing and playing the ending of 'River' by Ibeyi. They're chanting for Osun.

JAMAL puts on a Lil' Kim inspired outfit and yellow glasses.

Lil' Kim's 'Hardcore' poster appears on projection.

PARISS and AZIZI put on yellow jackets and glasses.

An instrumental plays and JAMAL performs

Lil' Kim's first verse from 'Crush On You'.

PARISS and AZIZI join him and become his hype men.

They all dance to the instrumental.

Another image of Lil' Kim appears on the projection.

JAMAL, PARISS and AZIZI pose.

They then take off their yellow jackets, glasses and sit.

I love Lil' Kim. I mostly love her for her raw and blunt lyrics. One of my all-time favourite Lil' Kim songs is called 'Suck My Dick'. She's rough. A boss. A legend. And I've noticed that her appearance and the way she presents herself has changed so much over the years, and I began to question why.

Lil' Kim has said that her previous boyfriends have always left her for, and cheated on her with European looking women, and she always felt that's something she could never compete with. She said that 'all my life, men have told me that I'm not pretty enough.' I never thought someone with such confident lyrics would have insecurities, but now I can see why. What she does to her face is her choice. I just wish she saw the beauty of her Black features and complexion.

A lot of music videos by rappers mostly include light-skinned women. And the amount of rappers that speak highly of light-skinned women, but diss those that are dark-skinned.

Like Kodak Black, who is a dark-skinned Black man who said, 'I just don't like my skin complexion. Light-skinned women are easier to break down.'

GlokkNine, who said in an interview he doesn't want a baby that's as dark as him. The worst thing about that interview is that a white man had to tell him that 'Black is beautiful'. Lil' Wayne in his song 'Right Above It' says 'Beautiful Black woman, I bet that bitch look better red.'

I used to make fun of Akua for her complexion, her complexion, her complexion and I can only imagine how it made her feel inside. And then I think about my relationships with Black men. White supremacy crawls and breathes. It crawls and breathes.

Every time I've been interested in a Black queer man, there's always been a dilemma. And the dilemma is usually a white or light-skinned man. I started to look at myself and think: what's wrong with me? Am I not beautiful enough? Should I cut my hair? What is it that they have that I don't? They're given so much more respect. These men are seen as boyfriend and hubby material, and for some reason I'm not.

I thought I was alone, but I've read articles and spoken to Black queer men that are going through the same thing. I had an emotional breakdown because I wanted Black queer men to love me as much as I love them. I kept getting angry and lashed out. I often woke up with so much rage, cried to myself and listened to songs about heartbreak. Beyoncé's rendition of 'Resentment' was on repeat. And each star in space looked down disappointed because I wasn't aware of my shine.

I was sat outside once with a Black queer man, smoking a spliff and drinking some white wine. And he tells me that he doesn't find Black men attractive. But every time a white man walked by, he thought they were fit and he wanted to fuck them.

And I know a Black man, who claims to be 'woke' and to love his people. We had a casual thing going, I then gained feelings and started to get all sensitive and I told him. He then thought we should just be friends.

But he's fucking a pretty white boy who works at an arts institution, second to the boss, has power to make things happen. And if this white boy gained feelings for him and wanted more, I bet you a lot of money that this Black man would give it to him.

There's clearly something they give that I can't. White dick must give some life support, or it makes them feel better about their Blackness. I'm probably too much of a broken mirror that reminds them of their trauma.

A beat.

Nina Simone's 'That Blackness' interview plays on projection.

'To me, I think we're the most beautiful creatures in the whole world, Black people.' – Nina Simone

AZIZI rings a bell five times. AZIZI and PARISS are playing music for Osun.

JAMAL begins to prepare a bath with honey, cinnamon, basil, perfume, yellow flowers, essential oils, Florida water and spring water.

He drops each ingredient into the bath and then stirs it with his hands.

He strips his clothes and enters the bath to cleanse himself.

JAMAL then gets out of the bath, dries himself and gets dressed.

SANGO

Spirit of Lightning, Wrath of God, Owner of the Double-sided Ax,
Spirit of Justice, Guardian of Twins, Spirit of Drumming,
Cosmic Dancer,
The Third King of Oyo Kingdom.

JAMAL lights a red candle and incense.

He then picks up and shakes a Rainstick.

PARISS and AZIZI start to chant 'Homage to Sango' and 'They Heap Insults On Sango' by Ella Andall

They're chanting for Sango whilst JAMAL starts to dance.

JAMAL stops dancing and they both stop chanting.

'Get Me Bodied' by Beyoncé plays. JAMAL starts to dance to it.

Beyoncé holding her baby twins, Rumi and Sir appear on projection.

JAMAL sits and the music fades out.

The first album I ever owned was 'B'Day' by Beyoncé. My Auntie Mara got it for me one Christmas. It's my favourite Beyoncé album. I never skip over a track because I love every single one. The thing most special for me, is that I feel like I've sort of grown up with Beyoncé.

All of her discography from Destiny's Child till now has come out through my lifetime.

And it's been great to see how she's grown over the years, as an artist and as a woman.

I'm very loyal to my Queen. I've seen her live twice and after each time, my love for her grew. I'm also very protective of my Queen. And if someone ever threatens her, I'm ready to attack.

He clears his throat.

Okay, I'm actually not that bad. I could care less if you liked her or not. I just feel people are a bit too harsh, and they go on like Beyoncé killed one of their family members. There's a lot of misogynoir going on. People don't like seeing Black women succeeding, whether they want to admit it or not.

I'm a member of the Beyhive, but I'm not delusional. Beyoncé is not above critique. For instance, a YouTuber called Chrissie, creator of Divine Dark Skin Magazine, critiqued a section from Beyoncé's 'Sorry' music video. Chrissie said:

'Beyoncé said: "Go call Becky with the good hair."

And you look at her in the scene on the video and she has Becky's hair on her fucking head.'

I think Black women should present their hair however they want to. But I can see what Chrissie is saying. And it's the combination of Bey's light skin, and whenever she has blonde hair that helps her cater to a white audience, which also helps her career. She knows how to play the game.

Yes, she can be problematic. But, who isn't? I know I am. Beyoncé then took a risk and started to talk about race, and a bunch of white people had heart attacks. A lot of her white fans prefer her earlier music, because that's when they could ignore her Blackness. And now, they can't.

I love me some Bey. How much do I love her? Hmm. Probably as much as Christians love white Jesus.

JAMAL looks at the white Jesus statue and then lays it down.

I would pray to Beyoncé before I would ever pray to white Jesus. I like the thought of them both being on the same level. For a Black woman to be as important as white Jesus is to the West.

In 2013, Beyoncé posed in front of white Jesus in the Last Supper painting and there was a huge uproar. I applaud her for that. I hope I can do the same thing one day, and piss off as many people as she did, if not more.

He smiles.

If I could be anything in the world, I would be a rapper. I'd be like a combination of Kendrick Lamar and Freddie Mercury. My stage name would be B.J. standing for Black Jesus.

Because I often wonder, what would this world look like, if lots of Black people owned pictures of a Black Jesus, instead of a white one?

Whenever a Mormon or some other type of Christian comes up to me, I say that white Jesus is a false representation and I'm not interested in engaging with something used to enslave my ancestors. Something that was violently forced onto to them. Something that has helped and continues to help white supremacy. Something that consciously tells Black people they need a white saviour, and that white Jesus is this perfect being, but Black people will never be perfect, just because their melanin is richer.

Throughout my life I've been told that Jesus loves me and I always said thank you, but now all I could think is slavery and colonialism, slavery and colonialism, slavery and colonialism.

I think about Black people, who will leave things in the hands of white Jesus. They hope he'll fix their issues, when he doesn't even care to listen to their prayers. Black saints exist, but it's so rare to see any bronze on the icons in Catholic Churches. There's Black Madonna, but there isn't Black Jesus.

The thought that the only way to a higher power or God is through whiteness doesn't sit well with me. White Jesus doesn't deserve a place in heaven, he should dive into a timeless blaze.

Uh oh! Blasphemy!

I get so much joy out of bashing white Jesus.

A beat.

PARISS picks up a marker and writes 'SLAVE' on JAMAL's face.

He lights a purple candle and incense.

I think if I were to be a celebrity, I might end up like Kanye. And I'm not even joking.

I feel like causing controversy is my kind of thing. I'm not always Team Kanye. I don't agree with his political views. And I also think he's too damn extra for wanting to change his name to 'Christian Genius Billionaire Kanye West'. But as the years have gone on, I now believe it was quite courageous for Kanye to interrupt Taylor Swift. He didn't mention race but, I believe his interruption had to do with it. Award shows are usually known for being racist as fuck, especially the Grammys.

Macklemore winning Best Rap Album over Kendrick.

Beck winning Album of the Year over Beyoncé.

Taylor Swift winning Album of the Year over Kendrick.

Adele winning Album of the Year over Beyoncé.

And no, their albums were not better. This is not up for debate! And what's even more interesting, is that Macklemore and Adele didn't think they deserved their awards.

Black people work so hard to be excellent. And there will be times where Black excellence will never be able to compete with white mediocrity.

*

One of the reasons I wanted to be a celebrity was because I thought they could do whatever they wanted, whenever they wanted. I saw them as gods with so much power. But that's not the case.

Colin Kaepernick was punished for not standing during the American national anthem.

He made this protest because he was frustrated with how Black people and other minorities were being treated in the US.

In 1993, Prince wrote 'SLAVE' on his face and changed his name to the Love Symbol because of the issues he had with then label Warner Bros. The press couldn't pronounce the symbol, so they started referring to him as 'The Artist Formerly Known As Prince'.

In 1996, he told *Rolling Stone:*

'People think I'm a crazy fool for writing 'slave' on my face, but if I can't do what I want to do, what am I? When you stop a man from dreaming, he becomes a slave. That's where I was. I don't own Prince's music. If you don't own your masters, your masters own you.'

I began to notice that Black celebrities in a way are just products, like they're modernly enslaved. Massa is the one that's in control of their contracts and usually has the final say. And if these celebrities founded their own record label, there's some chances Massa is still in control.

There are exceptions like Top Dawg Entertainment, founded by Anthony Tiffith, which is completely independent. But there are many others that are not.

AZIZI hits the drum after each statement, impacting JAMAL's body.

Roc-A-Fella Records co-founded by Jay-Z, Biggs and Damon Dash, owned by Universal Music Group. Their chairman and CEO, Sir Lucian Grainge, a white British man.

Odd Future Records founded by Tyler, the Creator, owned by Sony. Their chairman and CEO, Rob Stringer, a white British man.

OVO Sound co-founded by Drake, owned by Warner Music Group. Their chairman and CEO, Stephen Cooper, a white American man.

Aftermath founded by Dr. Dre, owned by Universal Music Group.

Bad Boy Records founded by P. Diddy, owned by Sony.

Dreamville Records founded by J. Cole, owned by Universal Music Group.

Murder Inc. Records co-founded by Irv and Chris Gotti, owned by Warner Music Group.

Cash Money Records founded by Birdman, owned by Universal Music Group.

They're just making money for Massa. Waiting for his approval, his applause. And here we have Jay-Z, who makes deals and plays ball with Massa. He's so desperate to keep hold of his Billionaire status, but doesn't see that his Black capitalist ways won't make a social change.

And then we have Kanye, he's a man, but he's not a white man. There's only so much he can do as just a Black man, and that's something he can't cope with.

OYA

Spirit of the Wind, Mother of Nine, Mother of the Marketplace, Warrior Queen, Strong Wind that gives birth to Fire, Mother of Change, Owner of the Winds of Heaven and Earth.

PARISS and AZIZI start to perform 'F.U.B.U.' by Solange. JAMAL wipes 'SLAVE' off his face.

JAMAL dresses in white clothing. He then sits to watch PARISS and AZIZI perform.

Once PARISS and AZIZI stop playing, JAMAL picks up a stool and moves it to centre stage.

In July 2018, I went to Trinidad and Tobago for two weeks and I'll never forget it. I went over to do research on slavery and sugar plantations in the British Caribbean. But I came back with something much more intriguing.

My 4C hair was living its best life because it got to spend so much time with Vitamin D.

I smoked weed and ate some mango with strangers. I got lots of mosquito bites. I heard an Indian man speak in an Indian accent, and then he jumped back into speaking in Trinidadian creole.

It was trippy as fuck!

It was so much fun to play spot-the-white-person, instead of spot-the-Black-person. In the UK, I often find myself either being stared at by white people, as if they've never seen a Black person before, or I'm constantly saying, excuse me, excuse me, excuse me. It's like they don't want to hear or see me. In Trinidad, one day I'm a bit lost, I go up to an Indian woman to ask for directions, and she looked at me and kept on walking. I thought it was quite amusing, because I was convinced that was something only white people did. I then asked a Black woman for directions, and she was more than happy to help me.

Overall the trip was positive, but there were sad and reflective moments. I saw a man who looked exactly like my Father. And I was so close to going up to this man and saying 'Dad, is that you?' I also saw lots of people who looked like my friends and family. One afternoon I saw a homeless Black man, who only had one eye. I remember wanting to take care of him and I still think about him now. In that moment, I was reminded of how I got to Trinidad with white people's money.

Every time my friend Arielle introduced me to her friends, she always said I was here researching with white people's money and they replied saying, 'Ayyy, get that money!'

I like to think of receiving my funding as getting some reparations. Special thanks to the British Council and Arts Council England.

One highlight was seeing Black people dressed in African attire on Emancipation. I saw an abundance of Black people so in touch with their ancestry. It rained dramatically, like there was a bitterness towards the day. But everyone was committed to celebrating the abolition of slavery in the Caribbean. Singing, dancing and getting extremely soaked. The joy from this day healed my mosquito bites. The feeling of blending in and not standing out was so refreshing, like the coconut water I drank fresh from a coconut.

I went to a queer-friendly nineties night and I saw a bunch of Trinidadians jumping up and down to 'Wannabe' by the Spice Girls. I couldn't believe it. And of course, as a queer man, I ended up on Grindr and Tinder. Just to see who's about. And who could potentially show me a good time.

I wasn't expecting much. But I was quite overwhelmed with the attention I was getting, especially from Black men.

I received a message one evening saying 'Hey, handsome' from a guy called Jonathan. Not a Trinidadian, but a Puerto Rican. An Afro-Latino guy based in Philadelphia. I was surprised that a good-looking Black man like himself was giving me the time of day. He's a dancer, charismatic, a great smile with refined cheekbones, facial hair, fully rounded lips, a nose ring on his right nostril, tattoos, curly crimson dyed hair and some lovely salted caramel melanin to top it off. We vibed. We both share the same Sun sign of Aquarius. Surprisingly, he knew about Leeds, because he knows Scary Spice, Mel B. He also taught me how to say some inappropriate things in Spanish and Portuguese.

One thing that was really lovely was him sharing his relationship with African spirituality.

His passion for it got me thinking more about my relationship with spirituality. I was keen to learn more about what else was out there. It doesn't seem like much, but it meant a lot.

But most of all, it felt so great to feel wanted. Jonathan said he would love to meet me and that he wanted me badly. I said show me how much you want me and he did.

JAMAL sticks his tongue out.

If I'm honest, it was one of the first times I felt that a Black man liked my complexion.

JAMAL smiles to himself and walks behind the altar table.

PARISS plays the wood flute and AZIZI makes background sound.

Whilst in Trinidad I learnt about the Orisas. They're deities from the Yoruba religion from West Africa. And were brought over to the Caribbean during slavery by the Yoruba tribe.

The Yoruba people made parallels between the Orisas and Catholic saints for their safety.

I was afraid to talk about the Orisas, because I didn't want to exoticize them, but I've learnt I won't be the one doing the exoticising.

I never thought it was possible to see a Black person, someone with my complexion, as a god.

I have Arielle to thank. She took me to some Orisa ceremonies where I had to take off my shoes, and wash my hands with holy water before entering the space. I saw lit candles and smelt incense. I heard call and response songs in Yoruba, backed by three bata drummers. The beating of the bata drums made my veins bounce with elation.

I saw people dressed in white or blue for the occasion, walking and singing in a circle anti-clockwise. I asked how long does a ceremony take and I was told that it takes as long as it needs to. I was so moved and inspired by this. It started from midnight with many energies floating around, an eclipse, a blood moon and the lion's gate portal.

And at no point did I feel out of place. Some nerves were present, because I was experiencing something new, but I got over that eventually.

I now make offerings to the Orisas, to invoke their energies and to honour them. I came across something that I saw myself in, something connected to my ancestry, something I felt was for me. I guess this is all I ever wanted growing up. All I ever wanted was to see myself.

PARISS and AZIZI stop playing.

JAMAL turns anti-clockwise and sits on the stool.

I'm back to reality now, back to attending art events and spaces where I play spot-the-Black-person, just like I did before. Even though I was struggling to come to terms with reality, it was nice to spend some time with family. My mother said I seemed different since coming back from Trinidad. The way I'm lighting candles and incense without her influence. And here's your reminder, if you don't want anyone to follow you once you leave this space, make sure you walk out anti-clockwise.

My mother still has her superstitions, but she no longer believes that our family is cursed.

She is now back to parting my hair, greasing my scalp with hair food, and we talk about men and she spills the hottest tea about some of our neighbours, whilst putting my hair in two-strand twists.

One Sunday after she finished my hair, I had to babysit my little brother Déshaun, as my mother and sister, Celeste, went to Church. He asked me, 'Who's your favourite superhero?' And I said Batman. I then asked who's yours, and he said 'evil Black Panther' a.k.a Killmonger. He likes Killmonger better because he looks cooler. He also said that he wants to be African because of him. He jumped up and down saying each line, going from a stereotypical American accent to a generic African one, and re-enacted each fight scene, from the kicks, the falls and even the explosions.

I sat and smiled for a bit, because I'm happy that my little brother can see himself in someone powerful, a superhero or even a supervillain. And I'm happy that my brother doesn't have to do what I did. Search for portraits of himself that don't exist.

Whenever I see myself, I know where I'm going. And when I don't, I'm trying to figure out where to go. I want Déshaun to take up as much space as humanly possible. And I'll encourage my fellow melanated ones to do the same.

Ase.

> *PARISS and AZIZI begin to chant 'Oya De' and 'Ere Asa, Oya La Mefa' by Ella Andall.*
>
> *They're chanting for Oya. JAMAL puts the stool next to the altar table.*
>
> *He dances to each Orisa and blows out their candles.*
>
> *He then goes into a prayer position.*
>
> *PARISS and AZIZI finish chanting.*
>
> *Blackout.*

> *'Sorry' by Beyoncé plays whilst JAMAL, PARISS and AZIZI dance out of the Palais.*

Songs

In order of appearance

1. 'Elegba 'go (ko) Lona – Make Way for Esu, Orisa of the Cross Road' by Ella Andall

2. 'It Bend Like Banana' by Vybz Kartel

3. 'Let's Go Crazy' by Prince (Warner Bros)

4. 'River' by Ibeyi (XL Recordings)

5. 'Crush On You' by Lil' Kim featuring Lil' Cease (Atlantic)

6. 'Homage to Sango' by Ella Andall

7. 'They Heap Insults On Sango' by Ella Andall

8. 'Get Me Bodied' by Beyoncé (Columbia)

9. 'F.U.B.U.' by Solange (Saint Records/Columbia)

10. 'Oya De' by Ella Andall

11. 'Ere Asa, Oya La Mefa' by Ella Andall

12. 'Sorry' by Beyoncé (Parkwood/Columbia)

WWW.OBERONBOOKS.COM

Follow us on Twitter @oberonbooks
& Facebook @OberonBooksLondon